FOR MEN ONLY

HOW TO LOVE A WOMAN
WITHOUT LOSING YOUR MIND

FOR MEN ONLY

HOW TO LOVE A WOMAN
WITHOUT LOSING YOUR MIND

BY JOSEPH ANGELO

MacMurray & Beck Communications
Aspen, Colorado

Printed and Bound in the United States of America
Library of Congress Catalog Card Number: 92-61177

Publisher's Cataloging in Publication
(Prepared by Quality Books Inc.)

Angelo, Joseph R., 1935–
    For men only : how to love a woman without losing your mind / Joseph R. Angelo.
    p. cm.
    Includes index.
    ISBN 1-878448-53-6

        1. Love.   2. Intimacy (Psychology).   3. Men– –Life skills guides.
I. Title

BF575.L8A5 1993   177.7
                                   QBI92-966

FOR MEN ONLY

HOW TO LOVE A WOMAN WITHOUT LOSING YOUR MIND

Table of Contents

*This book is dedicated
to all the women
of the world – –
only God knows how
you do it so elegantly!*

WARNING: DO NOT TAKE THIS BOOK SERIOUSLY

Loving a woman is not serious business.

PAY ATTENTION.

Loving a woman is not serious business, and therefore, nothing in this book should be taken seriously. If you take loving a woman seriously, you will start acting seriously, and the minute you start acting seriously, you create problems.

Serious business is waiting in your dentist's office and his assistant walks in wearing 6-inch heels and black leather. Serious business is the national debt and the trade deficit. Serious business is working for an asbestos company as an installer. Serious business is what happens before you are born; once you are here—forget it—it's a long water slide. Sit back and figure out how to have a good time.

Loving a Woman.

For you to love a woman without losing your mind, you must pay attention to the woman you love, just like you pay attention to business or any other activity you love to do: but a different kind of attention. This attention requires focusing less on activities and more on interacting. An ugly thought for most men, but we'll get to that later.

Who Is This Book For?

This book is for men who love women. It is for men who are tired of all the talk about how men should be, could be, and will be when they become enlightened, tofued, refueled, and generally more like women.

Who Isn't This Book For?

This book isn't for men who don't love women, men who want to control women, men who hate or abuse women. This book is not for women, children, astrologers, film critics, or guys who eat only what doesn't grow on earth. This book is especially not for the politically correct.

Men need not change to love women well. In the last twenty years the popular media has redefined men as: the cause of all women's woes, lowlifes, money hungry mongers, sex fiends, and now brothers in emotional impotency. Guys, forget it. Loving women is what men do naturally. No great problem exists between men and women.

WHY A BOOK FOR MEN WHO LOVE WOMEN?

If a man loves a woman, she is the single most important person in his life. Should we say that out loud? Yes. It's no big deal. It's biological, part of our nature—men like women. No, not just women's bodies—even though men love to look at women—men like the creature, the person, the soul in the body.

WHAT THIS BOOK ISN'T.

This book isn't the result of a survey of what many men think or an academic treatise about relationships. It isn't an objective study, nor is it the "truth."

TWO QUICK RULES FOR SUCCESS

RULE #1:
A WOMAN IS THE SINGLE MOST IMPORTANT PERSON IN A MAN'S LIFE.

Rule #1 is important, but right behind it is another biggie.

RULE #2:
MEN AND WOMEN ARE TOTALLY DIFFERENT CREATURES.

If you learn anything from this book, learn that women are different from men. Stop treating women as if they were men with tits and vaginas. They aren't. They are different creatures.

If you want to lose your mind, treat the woman you love as if she were just like you.

Loving women is difficult because they are so different from men. Women speak an entirely different language. They feel differently; they do things differently. But most of all, women perceive events differently from men. The simplest way to understand this is to think about sex. Men have an exterior probing, prodding, and pushy unit that gets very excited quickly and then fades. Women have a soft, warm, interior membrane that gets excited very slowly and stays that way for a long time. When you think about it, only love could allow these two units to connect.

WHAT THIS BOOK IS.

This book is a coaching tool for men. It starts with an allegory and then follows with tools and rules. This book is filled with over-generalizations, biases, opinions, ideas, and down-to-earth insights for men. Remember, lighten up, this is supposed to be fun.

JUST A NOTE ON READING THIS BOOK.

This book is not written: one, two, three conclusion. It is constructed like a Chagall painting—lots of pieces that don't fit together. When you think about it, you'll remember what you liked and might want to see again.

PART ONE
AN ALLEGORY

THE REAL STORY OF THE GARDEN OF EDEN

So God created the Garden of Eden in south Texas cattle country and plopped down Bob and Sally. Bob and Sally didn't know anything except what God told them, and that was everything, so neither could remember anything.

Bob had a herd of cows and was into yelling, ropes, and general hair-raising tricks. He chased his cows everywhere. Sally had a herd of cows and was into the milk cow scene. She petted them, milked them, sang to them, and made up names for them like Bossy, Bessie, and Moo-Moo.

Each night Bob and Sally got together and had dinner. Sally brought milk, ice cream, and sweet things to eat. Bob brought steak and ribs. Dinner was tasty, but boring. No talk, no touching, no sex, no bowling—just dinner.

Well, one day Bob decided he wanted more cows so he stole some of Sally's cows. He didn't think she would notice.

When he went to dinner that night he found a note from Sally: "You are a pig for stealing my cows. Fix your own dinner; I'm having apple pie." Bob, a rough and tumble cowboy, decided to make his own ice cream and get some milk for his coffee. He sat down next to one of the cows that he'd been chasing all day and grabbed one of her tits, but the cow kicked him in the head. The cow was not a happy Moo-Moo.

Bob couldn't believe what happened. He whined to no one in particular, "What did I do wrong? All I wanted was a little milk."

Hurt and angry, he did what he did best—remounted his horse and chased his herd with a new dedication.

The same night Sally had a hankering for a burger and some fries, but she had no beef. Bob always brought her the beef.

The more Sally thought about her craving for a burger, the more she realized that she didn't know how to do a lot of the things Bob did. She decided to change, and so she taught herself to yell, rope, and get her own beef. Meanwhile, Bob wasn't even watching. He was just waiting for her to come back.

Bob was having an ugly time. He didn't know what to do. No matter how long he chased those milk cows they didn't seem to want to give up their milk to him. He had his beef, but he didn't have any of the sweet things of life. And every time he spied on Sally, she was drinking milk and eating hamburgers without him. Besides that, he missed Sally, and he didn't know why.

Meanwhile, Sally was feeling a new sense of power. She had figured out how to chase, rope, and barbecue her beef cows all by herself. Although she felt good, she missed Bob, but she didn't know why.

Bob's birthday rolled around, so Sally decided to bring him his favorite ice cream—peanut butter-chocolate-pecan-hazelnut-brittle-fudge. Bob couldn't believe it. He thought she would never talk to him again nor would he ever eat peanut butter-chocolate-pecan-hazelnut-brittle-fudge again. They talked, ate dinner, and when they said good-bye, Sally stretched her neck and kissed Bob. Not a peck, mind you, but one of those Oh-God-my-spine-is-going-to-roll-up-like-a-window-shade kisses. Remember, Sally had changed.

Bob couldn't believe it. He kissed her back. Night fell; it grew cold, and Bob and Sally discovered why they missed each other so much.

They decided to camp together for a few days. Before Sally could say "moo-moo," Bob reverted back to his old cowboy self. He started telling her how to rope, that she should have brought more ice cream, and asking where his boots were. Sally was confused and didn't know what to do.

She was confused because in understanding where beef came from and learning how to chase the beef cows, she somehow understood Bob a little better. Against all her beliefs, she found that she liked acting like Bob. It was not as much fun as milking cows, but fun nonetheless. Bob, on the other hand, wanted milk and the sweet things in life, but he was not even in the slightest way interested in learning how to milk cows. He just expected her to bring him the sweet things of life. Worse than that, he didn't seem to want to understand her rhythm.

At first she felt hurt, then angry, and finally she realized she was bored with Bob.

She began dreaming about a man who knew how to milk a cow and make his own ice cream and other sweet things. A man who would appreciate how much she liked milking cows and making ice cream, a man who liked her roping and yelling, just as much as she liked and appreciated what he did and what he liked. A man

11

who didn't need her to take care of him. A man who wanted her just like she was—complex and exciting.

When Bob came back to camp that day, Sally was gone and all that she left was a note: "You don't get it; I'm not here to serve you. You are boring."

Bob felt stupid, and now missed Sally more than ever. For the first time Bob spent time watching Sally. He watched her talk to her cows; he watched her chase the other cows. He watched her milk, and he watched her barbecue. And then one night God visited Bob in a dream and said, "There are two kinds of cows. If you want what they have to give, you have to treat them differently."

Bob woke up and couldn't wait for sunrise. At dawn, he gently walked the milk cows away from the beef cows. He brought them good things to eat and talked to them; he even thought up names for them like Blackie, Brownie, and Spots. When the cows were contentedly mooing, he said goodbye and went to work chasing his beef cows. When he returned, his milk cows wanted to be milked, so Bob milked them. He wasn't good at it, but he still did it.

He was discovering Sally's rhythm. Weeks went by and Bob learned to do all the things Sally could do. Weeks turned into months and soon it was Sally's birthday. Bob made her beef stroganoff, sauteed veggies, and her favorite ice cream—bubble gum-cherry-vanilla-melon-twist.

Sally was surprised and glad to see him, but still a little pissed off. She couldn't believe how much he had changed. The more they talked the more she realized he had found her rhythm. It frightened her. She didn't quite know what to do but she remained calm, even though she felt wobbly inside. Just when he was leaving Bob said, "I have one more gift for you." Sally looked and wondered and then asked, "What is it?" Bob said, "My love. I love you Sally."

Sally couldn't speak. Bob left. Sally went to bed, and in her dreams God spoke to her. God said: "He solved the two-cow problem; now what are you going to do?" Sally woke and knew the answer. She got up, walked over to Bob's camp, and got into bed with him. They shared love.

———————•◆•———————

And so that's the real story of the Garden of Eden. The moral of the story is: in order for Bob and Sally to get along, Sally had to wake up, figure out what she was doing or not doing that made her so unhappy, make changes, all the while staying true to her feminine nature. And Bob had to find his masculine nature by not being the cowboy all the time. Sally became a woman. Bob became a man. Ever since Bob and Sally, men and women have been trying to figure out the two-cow problem, and lately they've been having a tough time. That's OK though, because God comes down now and then, speaks to men and women, and gives them a chance to understand each other if only in their dreams.

PART TWO
THE TWO CONCEPTION

PART TWO
THE TWO-COW PROBLEM

CHAPTER 1: (IN THREE PARTS)

PART 1: YOU CAN'T EAT BEEF AND DRINK MILK FROM THE SAME COW

Men used to understand their roles in life much better. Men were cowboys and that was that. Cowboys did cowboy things, and women were supposed to provide all the good things in life: "Honey, I'm home."

Life has changed.

Work and careers have become increasingly competitive, and it is more difficult to get ahead, let alone succeed. A man is forced to work more, and has less of a personal life than ever; when a man gets home, no "honey" greets him lovingly with beef and potatoes on the table. Honey these days is out roping, yelling, and chasing her own beef, and when she gets home she doesn't want to come within ten feet of the kitchen table, nor does she feel or act like "honey." No one is at home taking care of the milk cow. Just ask the kids about it.

What now guys? "Honey" isn't home and you don't know much about creating a personal life. Men are built and trained to achieve, compete, and bring home the beef, but they have personal needs that need to be fulfilled.

However, since "honey" is just as busy, facing the same kinds of competition—beef cow/achievement—as men are, many men have found a void in their personal lives. Their response to this emptiness is to blame the women they love — "You just don't understand."

Boys, wake up. Life is not going to get easier. "Honey" isn't coming home.

Now what's a guy supposed to do? Some men make the mistake of trying to develop the skills, attitudes, and behaviors of women — "their feminine side" — whatever the hell that is — big mistake. Most men's strongest inclination is to get back on their horses and chase their beef cows some more: marathon football watching, golfing everyday and on the weekends, working longer hours. All the while, they secretly hope that "honey will be home soon." No matter how clean the garage is or how low the golf score, honey isn't coming home. Ultimately men start to pout and blame honey for not giving them what they need and want: a personal life.

RULE #3:
IF A MAN WANTS A PERSONAL LIFE HE HAS TO CHANGE

Read it and weep. No ifs, buts, or maybes — today, men must learn to balance achievement-happiness with a personal life; a personal life requires milking the cow.

RULE #4:
YOU CAN'T EAT BEEF AND DRINK MILK FROM THE SAME COW.

RULE #5:
YOU CAN'T TREAT A BEEF COW AND A MILK COW THE SAME.

If you eat beef and drink milk from the same cow, the cow dies, your personal life disappears, your ability to compete suffers, and you're screwed.

One more time: if you try to get all life's rewards from achievement, at best, you get a kick in the head and sour milk. Reaping rewards from your personal life means using new words, feeling new things, and acting differently. No matter how vital the NBA play-offs are to you, no matter how well your dog is trained, no matter how big a deal you pull off — they will not give you the sweet things in life. A fruitful personal life does not revolve around achieving goals, creating products, and crossing finish lines.

A personal life starts with the fun, the talk, and the connection with the woman you love. But remember, she is not there waiting for you — she is just as busy, just as stressed, just as driven as you are.

Remember, it is not the job of the woman you love to provide all the sweet things in life. The game has changed and for the better in the long run.

CHAPTER 1:

PART 2: YOU STILL CAN'T EAT BEEF AND DRINK MILK FROM THE SAME COW

How do you balance the demands of achievement/competition and personal relationships?

You invest in two cows, a beef cow and a milk cow, and you learn to treat them differently. You chase the beef cow, but you better not chase the milk cow. You feed and milk the milk cow.

How? You develop the skills to be effective and successful in your work life, and you develop other skills to be effective and happy in your personal life.

A man's work life is whatever he does for a sense of achievement. That could mean building a city over a swamp or having a low handicap in golf; it could mean making $500,000 a year or having the best record at the tennis club; it could mean being a great independent film producer or a forty-year-old gym rat.

If you decide to strive solely for achievement-success, then all you get to eat is beef — there is no ice cream or the other sweet things along this path of life.

If you only work, focus on achievement and competition, no matter how successful you become, no matter how many people think you are the greatest, no matter how high you rank at the tennis club, no matter how many crises you avert, no matter how great your big wheel truck looks — you will be a very unhappy cowboy. Why? Because, you have denied yourself one half of manhood — the personal side.

A personal life revolves around the woman a man loves. The problem a man faces is putting aside all the achievement instincts that interfere with a personal life. But how does a man do that? He has to feel. Feel? Feel! Feeling: softening up, letting go of strict logic, goals, and the right way of acting. Feel: find the flow and dance between people who have equal rights and equal worth. Feel: connect with another human being.

When a man can feel, he literally and figuratively touches the people in his life. He reaches out and makes whatever and whomever he impacts important. He focuses his life on the pleasure of living right now.

Your success and happiness in life require a successful business life, and a satisfying personal life.

It's the task of manhood to harmonize these two sides of life.

It's your job to solve the two-cow problem.

If you own just one cow, you will try to get personal rewards from work that you can't get, or business rewards from your personal life that you can't get.

Personal rewards (ice cream and other sweet things) don't come from achievement-success. Nor do achievement-success rewards (steak and burgers) come from a successful personal life.

A man strives for both. Remember, there is no right way, but there is your way.

CHAPTER 1:

PART 3: NO MATTER WHAT YOU THINK, YOU CAN'T EVER EAT BEEF AND DRINK MILK FROM THE SAME COW

To Bob it seemed simple enough. Cows were cows. If you wanted beef, you chased cows; and if you wanted milk, you chased cows. Wrong. Milk cows and beef cows both fit under the larger category of COWS, but the two groups must be treated differently to reap their different rewards.

Achievement in your professional life and satisfaction from your personal life both require action, but you must use a different method of acting for each.

You can get a sense of achievement by doing anything: make furniture in the garage, run a Fortune 500 company, save the planet, convince people to smoke, sell drugs, or fight fires — doesn't matter what. Men are driven to achieve some sort of status, dominance, respect, or position in society as a result of their actions.

A man defines himself through action — what he does.

Anyone who thinks a man is driven by sex doesn't know men. Men love sex, but men are driven by doing things.

The woman in a man's life is his next most important focus. Then come his children, society, and spiritual growth in whatever order he shuffles his particular deck. Without a woman he loves and the achievement he needs, a man has trouble understanding exactly what life is all about.

A man seeks the challenge of fulfilling himself in all these arenas. He doesn't have to achieve external success in all these areas to be a man; he just has to know internally he has done the best he could do. When he knows this, he is at peace. He feels like a man.

Rule #6:

You cannot balance your achievement and personal life and please everyone.

If you can't please everyone then you have to make decisions about what you value. You know what you value based on how you spend your time and how you focus. Your masculine instincts will help you decide what you value. Think about it, if ducks use their instincts to fly to Florida for the winter, somewhere inside of you there must be a reference book just waiting to guide you.

Instincts do not come from a deck of Tarot cards or your personal astrologer. Instincts are part of your masculine nature that most likely have been in a coma thanks to this society's fads, fashion, and superficiality. Once you wake your instincts up, they will tell you how to read people, when to take business risks once you have done your homework, and when to push harder for success. Your instincts tell you to not believe the newspapers, TV, or the authorities.

Is time for men to wake up, and one of the fastest ways is to face the woman they love and see her as she is — totally different. But god, what a great difference.

CHAPTER 2: MEN WHO LOVE WOMEN

Many cowboys don't like women, much less love them. This, men, is the truth with a capital T. But even if you are among those who love women, you still probably don't know much about them.

Loving a woman does not require outstanding intelligence, sensitivity, or even understanding, although those qualities do help. Loving a woman is an awesome task because it requires your being a man.

A cowboy loves a woman because he wants something from her. What he wants and what she has to give are two different things. What a woman has to give is "it." But rarely does a cowboy get "it."

Most women, at one time or another, have fallen in love with a cowboy, but eventually they get driven so crazy, they fall out of love. And most men have fallen in love with many women who don't know how to get their own beef. That love is not "it."

"It" is that magical something that happens when a man loves a woman, and she returns his love. When a man and woman love,

25

nature steps in and injects both of them with instinct, passion, and desire — things that no one and nothing else can control.

"It" happens when a man and woman independently and mutually know and love one another. Independence is the key to getting "it." Dependence (needing Sally to milk the cow) leads to boredom. "It" means two people want to connect, not be in a relationship. Get it? Connection first. No relationship, no perfect picture, no "this is forever." A man connects and lets the connection spawn the relationship.

"It" is not permanent like a birthmark that stays there when you are fat or skinny, young or old. "It" is connecting, and connecting takes time, energy, and conscious choice.

"It" is a state of consciousness, a directing of focus toward another. "It" is not something you fall into. If you fall into love with someone, then you both have to dig your way out of the pit, and most often you dig in opposite directions.

"It" is what happens when two creatures with different rhythms connect for however long they connect.

"It" is the stuff of life.

Rule #7:
You don't get "it" if you don't give "it."

Rule #8:
If you can't receive "it" you can't have "it."

Rule #9:
If you can't sustain "it" you don't have "it."

A woman wants the man she loves. She does not need him. She doesn't want a cowboy though she sometimes acts like she does.

You know when a woman wants you because you can feel "it."

"It" is in her voice, in her eyes, and in her touch.

Let's just call "It" love. But if you start thinking Romantic Love, you'll be back on your horse acting like a cowboy in no time.

One of the big mistakes men make is to think that the way a man connects must look, sound, and act like the way a woman connects. It doesn't, it shouldn't, and it can't. A woman connects in harmony with her femininity, and a man connects in response to his masculinity.

"It" happens when two equally valued, sexual opposites connect. If you or the woman want to control "it," you can forget "it."

CHAPTER 3: BECOMING A MAN

oving a woman requires your becoming a man. Being a man isn't
n idea in your head, but a way of being in the world. It is easy to
e a man in the world if you understand some of the rules of life.

A FEW OF THE RULES:

RULE #10:

LIFE IS A GAME.

RULE #11:

THE RULES OF THE GAME ARE MADE UP.

RULE #12:

THE MEANING OF LIFE IS HOW YOU PLAY IT.

You become a man by knowing you're in a game, knowing the rules, and by using what you think and feel (masculine instincts) as a man to play the game. When you play the game fully you discover your manhood.

Remember Bob? Bob became a man when he learned to play both the personal part and the achievement part of the game. In order to do that, he stopped following the rules that said, "Sally's supposed to be this way or that way." Bob became a man when he no longer needed Sally to take care of him. Once he didn't need Sally to take care of him, he found that he could love her.

Loving a woman doesn't have to mean living in a house with a white picket fence, a dog, and a 9-to-5 job. Loving a woman is an experience, not a movie, regardless of what the cultural movie would lead you to believe.

RULE #13:
LOVING REQUIRES YOUR BECOMING A MAN.

The more of a man you become, the easier you find connecting with and supporting other people. You notice you feel secure in life, and don't need to dominate and control. A cowboy needs to dominate because he doesn't have a sense of himself. A man is powerful within himself; a man has strong values. He's thought about the world and about what happens around him. He is no longer afraid to be a man.

CHAPTER 4: THE PROBLEM OF BEING A COWBOY

Cowboys are unhappy — it comes with the cowboy suit.

There are many versions of the cowboy.

There is the lawyer cowboy, the rabbi cowboy, the sensitive cowboy, the new age cowboy, the hell's angel cowboy, the drug addict cowboy, the business executive cowboy — but underneath the different cowboy suits, most cowboys are the same. Everything in society tells men to be this or that kind of cowboy who does what he is supposed to do.

RULE #14:

SOCIETY TELLS MEN TO BE COWBOYS, BUT COWBOYS ARE DISSATISFIED AND UNHAPPY.

Cowboys are so unhappy because: they believe all the cultural lies that assert the "right" way everyone should feel, act, and think. It's a tough job to stop being a cowboy, since society only hints subtly about how to become men.

Deep down a cowboy gets pissed off when he's told what to do all the time. He may get pissed off and become an important member of society who tells other people what to do (a top hat and tuxedo cowboy), or he may rebel and say, "fuck you all" (a dropout motorcycle-riding, big-bellied hell's angel cowboy). In either case he's still a cowboy.

Cowboys haven't thought about their roles in life. They don't know how to take care of their personal lives, because a personal life means they have to stop being a cowboy and take off their cowboy costumes.

Cowboy costumes make men act more stupid than they really are (We might as well admit it to ourselves because sometimes we are pretty stupid.)

It's OK to do stupid things as long as you don't take yourself so seriously, as long as you don't think your stupid acts are "really cool." Everyone does stupid things, but cowboys don't ever listen to those around them who try to say, "Boy, was that stupid."

Some of cowboys' favorite stupid things are: driving fast to get to vacation spot to rest, getting angry and being right about their point of view when trying to get close to someone they love, giving speeches to their families and friends because they want to communicate. Mostly cowboys feel stupid when they don't act like men.

Men, not cowboys, realize men have had their asses whipped because they have been stupid about the wrong things. Men were wrong about letting the cowboys in power restrict women from chasing cows; men were wrong about letting the media take control over people's minds; men were wrong about believing they didn't have to be men. Men were wrong about trying to be the number one cowboy in a parade that goes nowhere. Men were wrong about not fighting for women and their personal lives. This is it guys. Either men have a good time with the women they love or they don't. And if you aren't having a good time, you are losing the game.

When you stop playing the cowboy role, you will discover that you think and feel like a man. It's that simple. If you are so busy being whoever and however society has trained you, you don't have time to be a man.

If you take the time to be the man you are, strange and wonderful things happen: your masculine values and points of view emerge, and you understand and appreciate other people's points of view. You discover how to love women and you finally understand that when a woman says she thinks or feels something, it means something totally different from what a man means if he said the exact same thing. You realize that the woman you love has a feminine point of view that will never mirror your masculine one.

You no longer react to women as if they were men with something wrong with them.

Think about Sally and Bob. She treated her cows as her friends. Bob chased cows like enemies. One way is not more right than the other, just different. If you want to make yourself totally insane, try and change her point of view or try and change yours.

RULE #15:
GET USED TO A FEMININE POINT OF VIEW.

CHAPTER 5: WOMEN CAN'T LOVE A COWBOY, AND COWBOYS CAN'T LOVE A WOMAN

Chasing beef cows leads to high achievement, and cowboys know how to achieve. Remember, achieving ranges from watching football every Sunday, playing golf every weekend, rebuilding old cars, to raising money for Israel. If all you do is "do," you are a cowboy. And it is hard to love a cowboy, and even harder for a cowboy to love.

Achievement-success may be your number one driving force, but if you want some of the nice things in life — love, ice cream, warmth, and human kindness — and a sense of the real power of your masculinity, you have to know when to stop achieving.

You don't have to stop for a long time, but if you want to love and be loved, you must develop a personal life.

Sounds simple. It's not. There is a rub, a conflict, a fly in the ointment.

You love this great woman — you love her like crazy. So you try to show it by giving her the fruits of your labor. How else would you do it, you are a man. You like it when your woman is proud of you.

But achievement comes from working harder, which takes away from the time you have to give.

The woman you love will grow angry because you spend less time with her. But it's not that clear because she wants two things simultaneously from you (she is a woman): (1.) your time (love, relationship, and maybe kids) and (2.) security (success). (I know it sounds a little old fashioned, but we're not talking Ozzie and Harriet.) We're talking about what a woman wants in today's world with the man she loves. She wants him to be doing something that requires mastery and passion so she can say to herself and to her friends, "Oh God, that is the man I love."

Guess what? Contrary to what she says, she will encourage you to go for success. Your success is extremely important to her. She will tolerate your postponement of feeding your own milk cow.

While she encourages you to achieve more she will also complain that you don't spend enough time with her, that you are insensitive that you are boring, that you are closed, and that you don't feel enough. This will profoundly confuse you. Wake up. She doesn't have your answer.

Here is where, how, and when you become a man.

A man uses his instincts to help him decide what he values. Your instincts lie dormant when you are a cowboy.

Rule #16:
Get to know your instincts.

You will need your instincts when the woman you love is caught between wanting a man to respect (an achievement-hero) and wanting a man who makes her the center of his life (the personal life hero). In either case, she loses. In both cases, you fail.

You are the one who must decide to build your personal life along with your achievement-success. There is not a right way to do it. But there will be your way.

This means you do things with the woman you love not based on accomplishing, attaining, winning, achieving, or giving in, being mothered and taken care of — but — are you ready for this? — sharing the experience.

You do things in a new way to be with her. You feed your milk cow, and she feeds her milk cow, and together you produce enough milk and good things that you share so you both are fat and happy.

Get it? You have to take the time to develop a personal life with the woman you love. You are a team of two, enjoying the process of sharing a vision about where the two of you want to go and how to get there.

Cowboys believe the illusion that pleasure comes when they have completed the race, reached the top of the mountain, finished the job, gotten the order, seduced the woman, or tied up the steer. All the while, the milk cow is starving.

If you wait for the goal line, you have missed the point. Stop waiting for your boss, your woman, your church, or anyone else to tell you when and if you can have pleasure, contentment, and balance.

37

CHAPTER 6: HOW TO BE INADEQUATE IF YOU REALLY TRY

Cowboys are cowboys because they don't want to do anything new. They want to do things their way, at their own pace, and with their goals in mind — a method that often works great in business, but is exactly the wrong way to do things in your personal life. If you want a gratifying personal life, you have to be willing to do what you don't already know how to do.

You must learn a new method.

Why? The activity is different. A man who doesn't try out doing new things doesn't have a personal life. New things means thinking new thoughts, feeling new feelings, and behaving differently. Most cowboys don't know how to have a personal life. They saddle up and chase milk cows, and wonder why they aren't getting what they want. Men don't get what they want because they want to do everything with the same method and approach that they've always used. Remember, getting what you want means changing first.

Rule #17:
A SATISFYING PERSONAL LIFE REQUIRES DOING NEW THINGS.

Caring for the milk cow isn't one of men's strengths. Learning to care for the milk cow means doing something new.

A woman who loves you wants to teach you to how to have a personal life so that you get what you need from it. Remember, the number one component in a man's personal life is the woman he loves, and the woman he loves, in most cases, knows about 1000 times better how to be personal.

If you don't learn to live with the woman you love, you don't have much of a personal life, and then you abuse yourself by feeling inadequate.

"Inadequate? Me?"

That's right, YOU!

All achievement and no play makes Bob an inadequate cowboy.

The emptier you get, the more you need the milk of life.

But to squeeze the milk out of life, you must feed your cow long before you milk it.

Get it?

Your personal life doesn't exist on its own, and it definitely is not the responsibility of the woman you love. Your personal life requires your doing new things. Remember Rule #17.

Cowboys fantasize about finding a woman who creates a person life just like Disney World — it just exists on its own and whenever they want it, they get entertained, good food, and then get to leave. Life doesn't work that way. Your personal life only works if you devote time to it.

Here is what usually happens: You want milk or a little ice cream with some chocolate sauce (something personal).

Surprise! You haven't been feeding the cow.

So where in the hell do you think you'll get this treat?

"You turn to the woman you love?"

WRONG! She isn't happy. She doesn't feel like giving to Mr. Achievement.

She has been waiting for the man she loves to pay attention to her like he once did. Mistake on her part, but this book isn't for women.

Then arrives every man's nightmare: the less you have to give, the more she wants you to give. Remember, the reason you wanted anything in the first place was because you were empty. Now you have a problem.

You think it's about your relationship. It's not. It's about you. You are empty, and you don't know it. And no matter how much work you do, it won't fill you up; you are chasing the wrong cow.

The more the woman asks you to give, the more you feel unrecognized, unappreciated, not respected, unloved, and inadequate. Guess what? You are the starving cow.

Unrecognized, unappreciated, not respected, unloved, and inadequate, you do what every cowboy knows how to do — you douse the woman you love by blaming her, just like you blamed your mom. "Where's my stuff? When's dinner? You just don't

41

understand me. What about me?"

Of course you don't know anything at this point, you're pretty stupid; you're a starving cow. So you just MOO and moo until the woman you love goes crazy.

Since you can't hear yourself mooing, you crank it up and accuse her of craziness, ineptitude, inefficiency, inconsideration, disrespect, and whatever else you can think of.

God, have you made a mistake. It is one of those cowboy mistakes women can't believe men make over and over but they do. But you make it, go on the attack, and drive her crazy.

In fact (great male phrase, because we always know the facts), she is beyond crazy; she is legally insane.

She is "legally insane" because in this male-dominated society she isn't thinking, talking, and feeling like a man. She has gone crazy trying to explain to you why you are starving. Have you ever tried to talk to a starving person? This is not an easy task. Men have never understood starving cows. She's insane because she's right but she can't quite say it clearly, especially because all the mooing and arguing and bad feelings confuse her.

You are wrong, but you don't see it. There she is — doing what doesn't work — trying to talk to you as if you were a woman while you try to talk to her as if she were a man.

At the moment of crisis, you are at the cusp of change — now either you go off your rocker or you let her teach you, via her craziness, how to feed the cow.

Here's a secret, big cowboy: when the woman you love seems the craziest, she wants to open you up and fill your personal life with herself. It won't be easy or logical, but if you stay afloat in the emotional hurricane you helped create, you'll reach dry land. She doesn't want to possess you; she just wants to penetrate you with her passion.

A man loves a woman's craziness because he knows he has, in part, caused it. Only when a man and woman muddle through their unhappiness do they learn how to feed their own milk cows.

So...enjoy the woman you love when she is crazy. It's part of the solution to your milk and beef dilemma.

PART THREE
FURNITURE AND BASKETBALL

CHAPTER 7: FURNITURE AND BASKETBALL (OR HOW TO LOVE A WOMAN WITHOUT LOSING YOUR MIND)

The woman you love has feelings you don't have. Repeat this sentence 8000 times a week. On top of that, she has reactions to those feelings that are completely foreign to you, and if you react to her feelings and her reactions to her feelings, you will lose your mind.

Often, a woman's reaction to her feelings seems to the man who loves her that she is speaking in foreign tongues and dancing with live rattlesnakes in her mouth.

Men go crazy when this happens because they think they have to do something. "Honey, don't you think those snakes are dangerous." You don't have to do a thing. Women have been going through feminine feelings their entire lives. They are not children with "boo-boos."

When a woman has a feeling about something and a reaction to what she feels, what she feels is her feeling. If you get involved in fixing it, her feelings will confuse you because there is nothing you can do with them. You can't tighten them, bolt them down, or straighten them out.

Think of it this way, you are outside playing basketball. She is inside rearranging furniture. (It sounds unfair, but go with it.) For some unknown reason, her moon is in Baskin Robbins or her numbers spell chocolate backwards and she starts crying. You go in the house, and she starts telling you her furniture woes.

You, the Fixer King, start moving furniture. You're not exactly sure why you move this furniture or where to put it, but you think she will feel better because you help her. Before you know it, all the furniture is outside on the basketball court, and she is shopping for new furniture and eating the advice of her astrologer. She feels ·better. But not because of you. Sorry.

You need to know that she didn't get better because you moved the furniture. She didn't get "better" at all. She had a feeling — an emotional experience that had a beginning, middle, and end. No matter what you did to help — you could have built new furniture, you could have painted the house, you could have walked around dressed in yellow chiffon, it doesn't matter — her feeling will end. You can make her feel worse, but not better.

Don't try to make it better even if you think you can. It is her feeling. Let her work it out herself. Be there. Pay attention — women don't need fixing, remodeling, or empathy. They want someone to listen to them and appreciate that they're experiencing something difficult. You don't have to understand it.

If you even attempt to fix her by taking in her feelings, they just float around inside you and make you crazy. If you try to fix her feelings you end up with furniture all over the basketball court, unable to play basketball, and resentful. All the while, she hasn't done anything wrong except have a feeling you thought you had to handle, control, or do something with.

But now, once you have taken her feelings inside of you and you can't do anything with those feminine feelings, you decide to save yourself by fighting them out of your system.

Now this is something men know how to do — they know how to argue, fight, and go to war.

Fighting and warring are useful tools at work, but they don't function well in relationships — they somehow interfere with the connection.

Standing up to the woman in your life is one thing, but fighting with her because you stupidly took her feelings personally makes her crazy and makes you a cowboy.

Remember you can't play basketball with her furniture all over your court. And if you don't play your game, you lose.

CHAPTER 8: SEX AND ICE CREAM

Nothing is simpler than sex. Women love sex. Men love sex. And yet sex is something totally different for men and women. That's not so bad except that society — the great unconscious sludge — has turned sex into some sociopolitical exercise with strong economic overtones. It isn't.

Sex is many different things. It certainly is what men and women do for fun. It just so happens, given the right conditions, women can have more fun than men. You create the conditions with a woman by giving her your attention. A woman loves a man's attention. Don't give her your attention because you want her to take off her pants. She will know it, even if she completely undresses. Give her your attention because it gives you pleasure. Once you give her your attention, she will give you access to what all women know and few men even dream about — sexual intimacy.

RULE #18:
WOMEN ARE MORE SEXUAL, MUCH MORE SEXUAL THAN MEN.

Mastering the fun part takes lots of practice. Sounds strange but most people don't have enough sexual practice. Their sexual knowledge and expertise equals the ability to paint by numbers. There is no art, creativity, or expertise. Once you master the fun part, sex will bring you to the doorway of intimacy.

Sexual intimacy is letting go physically, emotionally, and spiritually with the woman you love. Letting go is how you feed your milk cow.

Having fun and being sexually intimate are not mutually exclusive if during sex you get down and dirty, while you emotionally connect. Sex is personal in that you have to be willing to feel. Feeling is not limited to your penis. Feeling is what occurs between two people. It is a shared consciousness that you both can speak from. Women who feel, love sex, and women who love sex, feel. When you have sex, forget gender roles; instead, mesh your two souls. Enjoy connecting, the pleasure, and finding pleasure from each other. Women who don't love sex are out of the game. Sound too tough? Same goes for you cowboy.

Sex is not getting to orgasm. Orgasm is nice, but a vibrator will do the job for a woman, and your hand will do the job for you. Sex is connecting.

If your relationship isn't sexual that means trouble. Remember, sex is not about intercourse, sex is about being with the woman you love. Sex is about body closeness and physical intimacy.

Rule #19:
If you aren't sexual now, you'll only be less sexual later. Or, use it or lose it.

So let's think about it. If rule #19 is true, then you will lose your sex drive later if you don't develop a good and satisfying sexual relationship now. Just think about getting old and having forgotten about sex. Drag. Not fun.

One last point. Get ready. Sex is not love.

Rule #20:
Sex is not love.

When people go around thinking that sex is love, they become lunatics. If sex is love, then the longer most people are married the less they love each other. Not the case. Sex is fun and you have to practice to get good at it. Sex is more difficult than golf, tennis, or horseback riding, but most people would never think of spending four or five hours on a Saturday morning playing a round of sex with someone they love. They are too busy to practice and master sex. Nobody has the guts to admit it, and most will deny it. But then again, people used to think the world was flat.

CHAPTER 9: OTHER RULES TO KEEP YOU FROM LOSING YOUR MIND

Don't react to her crisis, or remember to keep the furniture in the house. Women have crises often and about many things. Don't forget, no matter what the crisis, it is just one crisis and she will get over it. But because it is a crisis she thinks she won't get over it until you do something about it. Don't. Most guys can't handle a woman's crisis, so in order to stop it, they stick their little hands in that emotional Cuisinart. Don't stick your fingers in her crisis unless you want her to feed you finger pâté, and you have a taste for your good intentions. If the woman you love is having a crisis, let her have it.

Stop trying to be fair. No two people are equal, so nothing is ever fair. There is no such thing as "fairness" in the universe. Instead of listening to themselves or their instincts about how to treat women or anyone else for that matter, many cowboys treat women like society tells them. Now that's a fine way to make yourself insane. Fairness is not the issue. Treat the woman you love and everyone from what is best inside you — your masculine instincts. When you do, you will feel that women are vital to your life and well being.

Don't fight. If you fight with the woman you love, you will lose.

Why? Cowboys and cowgirls love to fight. If you are with a woman who loves to fight — dump her. If you love to fight she should dump you. If you fight with the woman you love it will really piss her off. When women fight with men they love, they set sail on the sea of irrationality, and men foolishly swim out and drown. You drown because you keep trying to explain that what you said is not what she thinks it means. Get the picture. Why start it up in the first place?

Disagree but don't fight. When you disagree, either you are right and haven't explained yourself logically, or she is right and you are defensive or you are both defensive and hung up on some stupid point. Most often neither one of you is right, but you don't know how to stop and reconnect. If, however, you don't want closeness, get out of the relationship.

Don't take care of her. Care for her but don't take care of her. And don't expect her to take care of you. Mothers take care of children; adults care for each other.

Stop explaining, justifying, and rationalizing. Men often do what they want to do, and then try to justify their actions, which means they want their women to agree with them even if they don't. Cut the words; it is degrading and dehumanizing, because she knows you'll do what you want anyway. Women, not cowgirls, are straight creatures. Just tell it like it is and listen.

She has her opinion, you have yours; you aren't her boss anymore than she is yours. You won't change her mind — so don't try. And stop asking her to explain her actions. When you don't do what you want to do you are getting on the roller coaster to hell. If you decide to do something, do it; if not, don't. Cowboys sit on fences. Men take action and live with the consequences.

Don't shoot bullets when she shoots blanks. Your relationship with the woman you love includes every women's magazine she reads and her most vicious female friends. The magazines tell her she is a victim, and you are the abuser. And her friends love to tear you apart and use you for kitty litter. No "man talk" is comparable to women on a male search-and-destroy mission. These women talk like they want to annihilate what they want most — a man who loves them.

Their destruction is an illusion. Don't shoot back real ammunition at the woman you love when she shoots blanks!

It's part of the game — if you respond to her blanks with a full-fledged masculine attack, you're acting like a cowboy preparing to barbecue your milk cow. If, on the other hand, she means you harm, dump her.

Stop promising her your commitment. A relationship is about connecting. If you want a commitment, put yourself in a mental institution. If you have to make a commitment, make it to your business, your kids' homework, or washing the cars on Sunday. Connect with the woman you love. If you don't connect, why have a relationship?

COMPETITION AND COMPARISON: (TWO MAJOR ISSUES)

A woman knows what competition is, and where it belongs. She appreciates what you do — she doesn't compare. There are women who are more successful than you will ever be. A woman who successfully competes doesn't need to compare.

What you need is your passion. A man who isn't passionate about something might just find life a little hairy when he spends time with a woman who is passionate about what she does. She'll run him over like a big diesel truck hitting a paralyzed rabbit on the highway. (Not a pretty sight.)

If you're passionate about what you do, a woman who loves you will support you. It's a good idea to give support and passion back.

However, if she competes with you, then you have a problem. Watch out — you have an angry cowgirl on your hands.

Play your part in the relationship. A man and a woman who love each other both have roles to play in the real world and in the relationship. You better be clear about what is expected. Don't wait for magical solutions and psychic understanding. Play your part and let her play her part. Talk about your roles so you are both playing the same game. Remember, in the relationship there is no leader, only teammates.

PART FOUR
WHAT YOU NEED TO KNOW

CHAPTER 10: WHAT YOU NEED TO KNOW ABOUT WOMEN

What she wants: 100% of your attention when you are together. Pay attention to that sentence, it's a big secret. In fact, let's make it a rule.

RULE #21:
GIVE THE WOMAN YOU LOVE 100% OF YOUR ATTENTION WHEN YOU ARE TOGETHER.

When you are together, be there. Don't make phone calls, sort your mail, skim the newspaper, or tend the dog. Give her your time and attention; everything else is secondary. Don't tell her ever that she has your attention 100% of the time. She has been told that she is supposed to be your number one focus, but it just isn't true. If she believes she is the most important thing in your life, she feels betrayed when you focus on other things (competition). You feel unappreciated, and moreover, all the attention you gave her when you were together is lost.

What she wants you to be: She wants you to be her hero, he father, her good son, her bad son, her lover, her James Dean, he teacher, her girlfriend, her millionaire with free time and sensitivity her slave, her idiot, her genius, or any combination of the above.

Now that is all fine and good but totally unrealistic. This boils dow to: she wants you to be a man. You have to know, and let he know, that you are a man. Don't let her seduce you or frighten yo into thinking you must be different from what you are. Unless, c course, you want insanity.

She often doesn't know what she really wants. Even when she say she doesn't care about certain birthdays, anniversaries thoughtfulness, and such — she lies.

If she says everything would be OK if you were the way sh wanted you, she's wrong. If you were the way she wanted yo then you wouldn't be you, and she'd stop loving you, therefore r relationship.

Why she gets crazy: The woman you love gets crazy for tw reasons. The first is you. She feels crazy because the man she war — you — has inflicted pain on her, and she still wants to sper time with you. But spending time with you means undoing all tl hurts you inflicted when you were insensitive.

God, what a mess. By the way, even if you were perfect, she wou get crazy with you because of the bullshit other men have alrea put her through. Perfect or not, if you love a woman, you mu work through her craziness. She will love you for it.

The second reason a woman gets crazy is outside informatic What you say contradicts what other women, her frienc magazines, and books say.

She hears the basic message that the world is out of her contr dangerous, and she will end up alone. Furthermore, everyo victimizes her. She has been convinced that if she tries hard enough, she will someday get close to what she wants, and then she'll be old, and you'll dump her.

All this information destroys her and her femininity. She thinks she must be, simultaneously, thin, pregnant, beautiful, successful, independent, rich, career driven, in a good man/woman relationship, a good mother, young, mature, wise, and passionate — just for starters.

When you love a woman you take on an entire cultural campaign that, in summary, tells her she isn't worth very much. It hurts her. (Pain makes good consumers.) If it hurts her, then it hurts you. The woman you love will battle through the cultural war, but not easily. The war will make her a woman because, in order to survive, she will have to tear up all the fantasy pictures and disregard all the happy stories that tell her just how life should be.

No matter what you do the woman you love is going to go through periods of insanity based on what this culture does to women. You might get depressed, but this culture is kicking the hell out of her.

What do you do? Take care of yourself. Milk your own cow and stop waiting for her to give you the sweet things in life when she's busy trying to undo the Gordian Knot in her head.

It isn't that serious. Remember: loving a woman means loving her as she is.

A woman gets crazy in such a way that you can make her laugh, make love, get her to go shopping, or go get some chocolate ice cream (even when she thinks she shouldn't eat it).

If you are with a cowgirl who gets crazy, dump her. It's not worth the hysteria, withdrawal, punishment, and drama.

What she remembers: A woman will remember every derogatory remark you ever made and each one she thinks you said or heard you might have said about her and, especially, her body. She will remotely remember very few of the positive things you have said. She'll believe you said the good things because you felt like you had to, but you said all the bad things because you really meant it.

That she's an alien: Women are unlike any creature you have ever seen or will ever know. A woman is not a cat, bird, fish, dog, or any combination thereof.

A woman is especially not a dog. A dog likes to like you. A dog will lie around and fart with you, and let you feed it scraps. A woman isn't there for you, she is there with you. Big difference Mr. Pet Owner.

A woman wants you to like her for herself, not for who you think she is. Think about it for a minute. We don't take time getting to know women; we often just put them into one of our pet categories.

Her PMS: About three days a month a woman's mind, even to herself, is not quite right. While she experiences PMS, she has little consciousness of her actions and is legally insane on earth. If you take her PMS logic seriously, you are, with no question, a cowboy Sit back and praise God you don't have to frequently feel like you will explode from fluid building up in your body.

(What a great experience to look forward to once a month: You bloat, you are misunderstood, socially frowned on, overly sensitive and insane. Then your reward is hemorrhaging.) It makes sense to cut her some slack, especially since you have no idea how it feels Just assume that it isn't the best time she has ever had in her life.

Her lies: Women are the best liars in the universe. They lie so the can put up with the incredible abuse men, this society, and othe women inflict on them. No one knows why women put up wit such poor treatment. Think about it, even at our best we can b extremely trying much of the time.

Some basic lies: When you date a woman she will say the two of you are a perfect fit, and she wants to serve you in every way she can. She is lying.

She will say you are the best lover she has ever had. She is lying. (You can tell she has hit a new sexual level when she sees colors beyond the spectrum and speaks Cantonese with a French accent.)

During a relationship she will hint that once you marry her everything will be fabulous, and she will stop pressuring you. She is lying.

During your marriage she will tell you that you make her crazy. She is lying. She is really trying to work out all her conflicts with her mother and father, all her conflicts with society, through you.

She will tell you the most nonsensical insane things you have ever heard and assert that they make sense, and say that you're too insensitive to understand. She is lying.

She will tell you that you are the worst person in the world. She is lying.

Most of what a woman says is the truth to her. To you, she lies because you are a man. Remember, a woman is different from you. She feels differently, she thinks differently, and things have different meanings to her than they do to you.

Don't be offended by her lies. Don't believe what she says. Believe your feelings and your instincts. Don't believe accepted truths. Believe your body when you cuddle with her in bed.

If you connect with her energy, if you feel rested deep down, if you feel her accept your energy and you accept her energy—believe.

Everything else about truth leave for cowboys and the Daughters of the American Revolution.

One more lie. The woman you love will tell you she knows how you should act, feel, talk, think, and dress — she's lying.

CHAPTER 11: MORE RULES FOR SUCCESS

Make time. Let's say you've just worked 16 hours or you just finished mowing the lawn, building the garage, and painting the house and you come home. You feel like a piece of trash. You haven't even had time to urinate by yourself.

So what do you do when you get home? Get it straight cowboy, you save the last meeting for home and you put out. If you had one more meeting at work, if you had a date with a new woman — you would have energy. And don't ever kid yourself — she knows it! A man takes care of his connecting with the woman he loves by taking time and exerting energy when he gets home.

Remember, the woman you love thinks about your relationship about 100 times more often than you do.

You better start practicing "shiftability" — the ability to switch from the achievement mode to the personal mode of living.

If you don't you become an asshole. Nothing feels worse than knowing you're being an asshole with the woman you love. Cowboys don't know and don't care to know.

Play the flow. Living with a woman makes living so exciting. If you live with a woman, give up the idea of "your way." Also give up the idea of "the right way." Learn to play the flow.

Talk. Men like to give speeches, spout, reveal theories, understand, and come to conclusions. This bores women (and other men).

Talk is what women love and want. During talk no conclusions are drawn; there is give-and-take. You are "just talking." The talking itself is important. Talking is connecting. Talking means interchanging.

Think about all the "important" things you've ever said or other people have said. Where did all the important talk go? Into the air that it was.

Stop talking about important things — just talk. Talk can be surprisingly interesting. Talking does not mean gossiping and catching up on all the latest news.

Listen to her and respond to what she says and feels. Don't lecture, preach, or categorize.

Learn how to kiss and touch when you talk.

Women are suspicious of talking with men because men aren't used to it. Women are used to arguing with men.

Communicate. It is not that difficult for men and women to communicate more effectively. For starters, stop apologizing, back stepping, being overly cautious, and generally unmanly, and start listening, feeling, and connecting.

Kiss and touch. Kissing and touching is vital to your life. You need it and so does the woman you love. Men often think that kissing is a prelude to coming. Forget it, coming isn't the issue in life. If it were, then life would be simple. Kissing and touching lead to connecting.

Share the details. Many women love details — details about themselves, you, and your relationship. Most men don't.

If you want her attention, remember details. Remember what she wore on your first date, what she ordered at your first dinner, and what she said the first time you had sex. Guys, this is the truth. Nearly impossible but the truth.

Etiquette. Open doors. Wait for her. Treat her with delicious respect and consideration. Most likely she treats you this way, but you don't know it.

Time and dressing. It is true that most women take much more time to dress than men. Why? Think of all the stuff they must do. Dressing is not an event for men, for women it is trial by fire. If you rush her, you will pay for it later. It is cost effective to sit back and enjoy yourself. She'll get there anyway, so back off.

Focus on her. Big secret here guys.

If you give her your focus, you will have a woman who loves you passionately.

Focus means you track what she says and hear what she feels.

Focus means you feel her and what she feels.

Focus means you take her into your body.

When she hurts about something — focus. When she is happy — focus.

Remember, each moment is "it." Focus in the present and let the moment go so you stay with the next emerging moment.

Turn the TV off. One of the worst things in a relationship is the TV. TV damages relationships; it helps destroy them. If the two of you spend more time watching TV than talking to each other, you'll soon be in a soap opera yourselves.

Rule #22:
TV IS DANGEROUS TO A PERSONAL LIFE.

Pay attention — TV is dangerous.

Make it erotic. If you can plan a successful business meeting, you can plan your personal life. Plan weekends, vacations, and sensual dinners for two. A cowboy wants a mom to take care of his life. A man makes his life happen.

If the woman you love makes excuses about your plans together, push them until she remembers eroticism with you.

If she doesn't remember, she wants out of the relationship.

Send her cards and flowers. If they don't affect her, review your past with her because the relationship could be over.

Call her on the phone. Put one line messages on her answering machine. Make her laugh.

Reveal your fears. A woman will share your fears, problems, or stress, but not too much fear, too many problems, or too much stress. Learn to take care of yourself and your life. She wants to share, not repair. So when you open up, don't flood her with the broken appliances of your life.

CHAPTER 12: WHEN YOU HAVE TO BE THERE:

Whenever you are there.

Birthdays.

Childbirth.

Her major tooth surgery.

Her abortion.

Her first night home from a new job.

When someone close to her dies.

Menopause.

Really big birthdays — 30, 40, and 50.

When she cooks something while you're home. Don't watch TV or read the newspaper. Remember, time with the woman you love means feeding your milk cow.

Holidays.

When she is stressing out.

Whenever she is premenstrual and commercials make her cry.

CHAPTER 13: WHAT YOU NEED TO REMEMBER

Kisses.

Her birthday.

The day you got married.

The day you got engaged.

The day you first dated.

The day you first had sex.

When she gets her period.

How long her period lasts.

When she gets PMS.

How long her PMS lasts.

Hugs.

The birthdays of your children.

All important holidays.

The color of her eyes.

The color of her hair.

Kisses.

Her dress size.

Her shoe size.

Her ring size.

Her bra and panty sizes.

Kisses.

Her nightgown size.

The flowers she likes.

Hugs.

What she wants most in the world that you can't afford.

What she wants most in the world that you just can't afford.

What she wants most in the world that you can afford but to buy would be really painful.

What she wants most in the world that you just can afford and that you would love to give her.

Hugs and Kisses.

And about 15,000 other things, but you can't and most likely won't remember what they are. Try.

You can always remember to hug and kiss a lot.

CHAPTER 14: THE RED LIGHT
IS FLASHING – – –

When you are afraid of her.

When she is afraid of you.

When you are so afraid, you don't bring up touchy subjects.

When she is so afraid, she doesn't bring up touchy subjects.

When she is always angry with you.

When you are always angry with her.

When she is always wrong.

When you are always wrong.

When you don't spend enough time together.

When she doesn't care if you are sexual or not.

When either of you sleep every night on opposite sides of the bed.

When she sleeps late and goes to bed early.

When you stay up late and get up early.

When she is always sick.

When you are always sick.

When she is always late.

When you are always late.

When you don't have enough sex.

When she doesn't talk.

When you don't talk.

When she forgets your birthday.

When you forget her birthday.

When you don't want to do the things she used to love doing for you.

When you don't want to do the things you used to love doing for her.

When she doesn't laugh at your jokes.

When you don't think she's funny.

When she doesn't think you're smart.

When you don't think she's smart.

When she doesn't want to talk.

When you don't want to talk.

When she says she loves you, but she isn't "in love" with you.

When you are not attracted to her, but you love her.

CHAPTER 15: WHAT YOU GET WHEN YOU ARE A MAN WITH A WOMAN

You get someone who loves you.

You get someone who can take in all your energy, passion, craziness, lust, caring, stupidity, and still love you.

You get someone to take in, and love, and do good things for.

You get to take in the illogical, emotional, upsetting, crazy, wonderful, passionate, sensitive thoughts and feelings that the woman you love will give you.

You get to rest.

You get to laugh.

You get someone who laughs at your jokes.

You get to stop being so important.

You get to be vulnerable.

You get to give.

You get to listen to all her complaints about the world.

And you get to listen to all of her irrational joy.

You get someone who listens to all your theories and complaints, and likes listening to you.

You get to cook.

You get to do the dishes.

You get someone who compliments and coaches you.

You get to be good.

You get to be appreciated.

You get to appreciate.

You get to give sexual love.

You get to receive sexual love.

You get to have your spirit opened wide.

You get to open wide the spirit of the woman you love.

You get to wake up every morning next to the woman you love.

CHAPTER 16: UNDERSTANDING WOMEN

Forget it!

Men will not now, nor in the near future, understand the women they love.

Love your woman — don't try to understand her. You can't, you won't, and even if you could, she wouldn't like it.

If you could, even marginally, understand yourself during your lifetime, you would be lucky.

An understanding of women has never occurred in the history of humankind nor will one occur in the future.

How can you understand someone that you were told "came from one of your ribs"? Who made that up?

A woman changes all the time, and if you want to understand anything — understand change. What you think you understand today, changes tomorrow.

If you swim with the flow of her changes you play your part as a man. Reread the last sentence. That allows you to love her: you're a man while she's a woman. A woman lights up your life like no fireworks finale can.

Cowboys want to, and think they can, understand women.

Men know they can't and they don't care; they love instead.

CHAPTER 17: THE FINAL CHAPTER

o, here we are. Bob and Sally snuggle in bed and you, just one
nore cowboy, wonder what the hell to do. It's really not that hard,
f you are gentle with yourself and think about it.

Women are different, really different, and men keep trying to relate
o them as if they were men. Each time you do that they don't like
. When women don't like something, they often overreact because
hey are so used to being mistreated.

is true that lots of women in the world are terrible bitches, but
most didn't start off that way or create a plan to be a bitch. For right
ow, men have it in their power to make women realize they are
ot trying to remake them and that they love them. This is a good
ning. Women make men's lives livable.

ut to connect with women, men have to learn how to take care of
eir own personal lives. The minute you don't need a woman to
ke care of you, you no longer need to control her to guarantee

yourself the sweet things of life. Instead, you are free to be yourself with a woman who is being herself. You both have something to give and receive — life.

If you choose manhood instead of cowboyhood, you just might discover how exciting and dangerous, great and challenging, delightful and peaceful life with the woman you love can be.

Good luck until we meet again.

BIOGRAPHY

Joseph Angelo attributes everything he knows about women to his mother, five sisters and all the women he has ever loved. He writes from experience, from what he has learned, heard and seen. His two new books **For Men Only: How to Love a Woman without Losing Your Mind** and **Lifequake: What to do in the Worst of Times** are both written in a new style that is designed to inspire people to be honest with themselves.

INDEX

Values, importance of identifying, 23, 30

Values, importance of identifying, 23, 30

Order Form

(For credit card orders, please call 1-800-233-3792)

Quantity

For Men Only
by Joseph Angelo, ISBN 1-878448-53-6
_____ Paperback ($9.95 x number of copies) $ _____

Lifequake
by Joseph Angelo, ISBN 1-878448-55-2
_____ Forthcoming—order will be kept on file

**Changing Woman,
Changing Work**
by Nina Boyd Krebs, Ed.D.,
ISBN 1-878448-56-0
_____ Hardcover ($22.95 x number of copies) $ _____

Some Mid-night Thoughts
by Mary Hugh Scott, ISBN 1-878448-52-8
_____ Paperback ($12.95 x number of copies) $ _____

The Passion of Being Woman
by Mary Hugh Scott
_____ Hardcover ($19.95 x no. of copies), $ _____
ISBN 1-878448-50-1

_____ Paperback ($12.95 x no. of copies), $ _____
ISBN 1-878448-51-X

Shipping ($2.50 for 1st book, $1.00 for $ _____
each additional book to same address)

Colorado residents add 3.3% sales tax $ _____

Total $ _____

Name _____

Address _____

City, State, ZIP _____

Phone _____ (for order clarification only)

Make checks out to MacMurray and Beck and send to:
PO Box 4257, Aspen, CO 81612.